# RUSSELL

# RUSSELL

Amy Buskirk

BARNES
&NOBLE
BOOKS

NEW YORK

This edition published 1997 by
Barnes and Noble Inc.,
by arrangement with Saturn Books
Limited.

1997 Barnes and Noble Book

Produced by Saturn Books
Kiln House, 210 New Kings Road
London SW6 4NZ

Copyright © 1997 Saturn Books Ltd

ISBN 0 7607 0048 6

Printed in Singapore
M 10 9 8 7 6 5 4 3 2 1

# CONTENTS

# INTRODUCTION

Charles Marion Russell — the 'Cowboy Artist' — was the quintessential self-made man who followed his dreams and found success. Born with a love of the West and the talent to portray its landscape and people, Russell created a stunning collection of paintings and sculpture and made a fortune in the process. Among the thousands of books, paintings, photographs and films that take as their subject the Old West, Russell's work portrays a knowledge, humor and skill that few others have achieved. He managed to evoke the raw excitement of cowboys' lives in paintings such as *The Herd Quitter* (1897) and the *Just a Little . . .* series (1898), but he could also focus his talent on the tragic lives of the West's indigenous population. Russell's painting *The Fireboat* (1918) poignantly hints at the pain and loss the Native American tribes of the West would face with the coming of the white settlers.

From the cowboy's dusty Stetson and shiny spurs to the Indian's feather headdress and beaded moccasins, Russell captured an era that was to die within his lifetime. Almost 100 years have passed since overgrazing and farming brought an end to the cattle drives of the Great Plains, since the US government and its military destroyed Native American culture, and since highways and cities replaced wagon trails and open ranges. However, Charles Russell's legacy provides late-20th century viewers with a unique and beautiful insight into that past world known as the Old West.

Mary Elizabeth Mead and Charles Silas Russell welcomed their son Charles into the world on March 19, 1864. St Louis, Missouri, Russell's hometown, undoubtedly contributed to his lifelong passion for all things Western. In the latter half of the 19th century the city was busy earning its nickname 'Gateway to the West'. Its streets bustled with fur trappers who trekked between St Louis, the headquarters of American fur trading, and the wilderness where they acquired their pelts. The grand Mississippi River was equally crowded with steamboats transporting would-be settlers, cowboys and prospectors just north of the city to the Missouri River and the beginning of their journey west.

Charlie — as he was called throughout his life — reveled in the excitement of the city's riverfront. At the age of 12, this 'wharf-rat' wiled away his school days on the docks listening to the astounding stories of the West told to him by riverboat men, fur traders and plainsmen. Russell's parents soon discovered his deception and sent him back to the schoolhouse, but they would find it impossible to curb his Western fantasies, and part of his inspiration came from his father's ancestors.

Russell's family had lived in St Louis for more than 60 years and was among the most prominent clans in the relatively young city. Silas Bent, Russell's paternal great-grandfather, moved to St Louis from Massachusetts in 1804 and served as chief justice on the Missouri Supreme Court. Charlie's father emulated his grandfather in middle-class respectability as a successful businessman who could afford to house his wife and six children in a fashionable home in Oak Hill, a suburb of the city. But it was not with these conservative figures that Russell identified; he was far more impressed with William Bent, his great-uncle and the first white settler of what was to become Colorado. As a young boy, Russell would gaze at the family portrait of Bent and imagine himself clad in buckskin, fighting Indians and exploring the frontier just as his adventurous forefather had done 50 years before.

When Russell wasn't feeding his interest in the West with trips to the waterfront or daydreams about his great-uncle, he was reading newspaper accounts of the US Army's exploits in the Indian Wars or Western adventure novels. Like children today, Russell and his friends enacted the stories they heard and read. In his grandfather's woods, the streambed expanded to become the Grand Canyon; bushes became bears; calves grew heavy coats to become buffalo; and with chicken feathers and paint the boys transformed themselves into Indians who scalped and burned their sisters' dolls at the stake. On his much-loved pony Jip, the young Russell tore about the countryside dreaming of the day he would ride across the Plains far from the confines of St Louis and his family home.

RIGHT: Charles Marion Russell photographed in his studio in 1923, while painting *The Buffalo*.

LEFT: Russell dressed as an Indian.

His childhood relationship with Jip was the beginning of a lifelong equestrian love. The knowledge and respect that he possessed for horses shines through in the paintings and models he would later create. *The Bucker* (1904), *The Jerkline* (1912) and *Changing Outfits* (1916) are just a few of the hundreds of examples of Russell's skill at portraying the animal's willful energy, grace and intelligence.

Paired with young Russell's fascination with the West was his equally strong passion for drawing and

modeling. His talent became apparent when, at the age of four, he sculpted an American eagle with only a book illustration for a guide. At about the same time, the young artist was often punished with a spanking for using his mother's clean steps, walls and hearths as a medium on which to draw cowboys and Indians. As the boy grew older, the Russells encouraged their son's artistic inclination by supplying him with beeswax that he would mold into remarkable animals and human figures. Russell won his first of many public accolades (a blue ribbon)at the age of 12 when his father entered one of his sculptures, a bas-relief of a mounted knight, in the St Louis County Fair.

Like many creative people, Russell chafed under the reins of authority. Perhaps this is why he longed for the West's open ranges and hated the confines of school so much. Russell's father was determined that his son should have a college education that would enable him to join the family firebrick manufacturing business, but much to the senior Russell's displeasure, his son was more interested in using clay to produce models of cowboys and Indians than in making bricks. In a final effort to cure Russell of his passion for the West, his parents sent him to a New Jersey military school when he was 14 years old.

After only one term, during which Russell infuriated his teachers with his lack of attention and poor study habits, his parents agreed that he would gain little in returning to the school. Instead, his father decided to encourage the lesser evil of Russell's twin obsessions and arranged for his son to attend art school. Russell lasted just three days. Faced with a traditional instructor who insisted that his students draw the plaster foot he placed in front of them, Russell rebelled yet again. He longed to draw the active, exciting subjects of his imagination, not some immobile, dusty foot. The brief time he spent at the St. Louis art school was the only directed art education Russell was to receive. His disparaging opinion of the formal study of art remained unchanged throughout his life, and he had no patience for those who thought studying abroad was necessary for an artist. Russell argued: 'I don't see how a Dutchman or a Frenchman could teach me to paint the things in my own country.' Russell's lack of formal education is evident in the appalling spelling found in his personal correspondence, but academic training was unnecessary for the life he desired. He wanted to experience and learn about the West first hand, and upon turning 16 Russell had the opportunity to gain this knowledge.

By this time Russell's father had become resigned to the fact that his son's destiny did not include a respectable life in the city, so he arranged for Russell to travel to the West 'in the right way' with a family friend, Wallis W. (Pike) Miller. Miller escorted the excited boy on the new Union Pacific and the Utah and Northern railroads to Red Rock, Montana Territory, and then on a stagecoach to Last Chance Gulch, the town that was to become Helena. One can imagine the young boy's feelings on this journey; he was finally seeing the land he had dreamed of all his life. Perhaps unsurprisingly, the 4,000-strong settlement of Helena failed to meet Charlie's childhood expectations. The town was crowded with Flathead Indians collecting their government rations, and Russell later remembered:

'I was sure disappointed right there. 'Course I didn't say nothin' to nobody 'bout it, but I'd expected to see them Injuns wearin' war-bonnets and all the white men wearin' long hair an' buckskin shirts. At least that's what Ned Buntline an' all the rest of the writers had said 'bout 'em an' that's the picture I'd formed.'

By the spring of 1880, when Russell arrived in the Montana Territory, the Great Plains were undergoing a dramatic transformation, which no doubt contributed to his disillusion. Between 1871 and 1883, hunters would kill 40 million buffalo for their hides and leave just over 100 alive. Along with the near-extinction of the buffalo came that of the Plains Indians who relied on the beast for everything from their food to their blankets, teepees, saddles and weapons. Russell mourned the loss of the buffalo and the life it sustained and would later use paintings such as *Where Great Herds Come to Drink* (1900?) and *When the Land Belonged to God* (1914) to document the majestic animals that were so thoughtlessly slaughtered. He would also denote his remembrance with a sketch of a bleached buffalo skull that appeared with his signature on almost all his work.

The encroachment of settlers was also changing the open landscape of the West. Since the passing of the Homestead Act of 1862, farmers could claim up to 160 acres of land if they erected houses and fences on the property. With the coming of railroads in the 1870s and 1880s, the steady stream of farmers increased and their barbed wire fences would eventually contribute to the end of the cattle drives and the cowboy. With his sketch *Trails Plowed Under* (1900?) Russell captured the clash of the two ways of

RIGHT: Charles Russell on Neenah, 1906. Watercolor on paper, 12 x 9 in.

Compliments
OF CM Russell
To Mr & Mrs A J Trigg

life. In later years, he complained bitterly about the farmer: 'Where we used to have grass, weeds grow now. Since the coyote got thinned out, there's lots of gophers . . . [The farmer] plants corn an' gets tumbleweeds. Damn him! It serves 'im right.'

Nevertheless, despite his initial disappointment, the young Russell quickly grew to love the territory that still held many adventures, wondrous sites and mysteries, and he never faltered in his commitment to recording the majesty that he encountered in the

ABOVE: Russell and Jack on horseback.

RIGHT: Self portrait, 1900. Watercolor on paper, 12⅜ x 6⅞ in. Buffalo Bill Historical Center, Gift of The Charles Ulrick and Josephine Bay Foundation, Inc.

Complements
of
C M Russell
1900

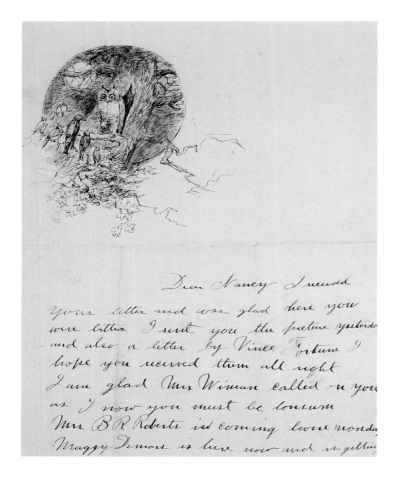

West. From the moment he arrived, he adopted Montana as his home and would only leave it for brief periods throughout the rest of his 46 years.

Russell's first job in the West, as a sheepherder on Pike Miller's ranch, failed to provide the excitement the teenager had anticipated. Sheep were slower and less romantic than the cattle Russell longed to herd, and his disinterest made him a poor hand. Charlie laughingly remembered that Pike 'couldn't buy sheep fast 'nough. I'd lose the damn things as fast as they'd put 'em on the ranch.' But it was difficult for his employers to be angry with him; Russell — known as 'the Kid' at this time — provided much amusement with his sketches and models. His wit, artistic skill and comical caricatures were a welcome relief from the monotony of the isolated settlement.

Quickly growing restless, Russell left Miller's sheep ranch in pursuit of a job as a cowboy, but was sidetracked for two years by a woodsman named Jake Hoover. Russell later recalled their first meeting on the banks of the Judith River: 'I couldn't help feelin' that the big heart of this old trapper an' hunter understood me better'n anyone I'd ever met an' he was goin' to be my friend.' Hoover's rough-hewn log cabin stood along the isolated South Fork of the Judith and offered few of the amenities Charlie had known as a child, but it was there and in the surrounding woods that Charlie laid the foundation of his immense knowledge of the West and its animals.

For Charlie, 'ridin' with Jake was like a chapter of [his] favorite book of the Rocky Mountains.' In truth, Charlie was no hunter, he preferred to capture the bears, beavers, deer and elk that abounded in the valley in his art, rather than in traps, but by skinning Hoover's game, he gained a familiarity with animal muscular structure that would become useful in his paintings and sculpture. *Crippled But Still Coming* (1913), *Meat's Not Meat 'Till It's in the Pan* and *Mountain Mother* are just a few of the works that would later benefit from Russell's two-year study of mountain wildlife.

In portraying the West as an artist, Russell was carrying on a tradition that had begun shortly after the United States purchased the Louisiana Territory from France in 1803. Although artists like Charles Bird King (1785-1862) painted what they imagined to be the West from the comfort of their eastern studios, others were eager to witness the wonders of America's new property first hand. In the 1830s, George Catlin (1796-1872) journeyed 1,800 miles throughout the West and recorded the culture of the Native American tribes he encountered in over 500 paintings. Russell had seen Catlin's work in the many traveling exhibitions that stopped in St Louis, and his own work is similar to Catlin's in its portrayal of Indians as human beings rather than savage, unthinking creatures. The influence of Alfred Jacob Miller (1810-74), who also spent time in the West in the 1830s and whom

*Maney snows have fallen since the Black feet an Sioux smoked. and the grass has grone long in the trail betwene there fires but if Short Bull comes to the lodg of the Antilop the pipe will be lit an robes spred for him the Antilope has spoken*

HO-HO-HAYE

.AH-WA-COUS

ABOVE LEFT: "Dear Nancy..." – an 1896 letter from Charles Russell to his wife, the former Nancy Cooper.

ABOVE: "Maney Snows Have Fallen..." – a letter from *Ah-Wa-Cous* (Charles Russell) to Short Bull. c. 1909-10, pen and ink and watercolor on paper, 8 x 10 in.

Russell admired as a child, is also apparent in Russell's *oeuvre*. Although his active and detailed style differs from Miller's atmospheric renderings, Russell was inspired by Miller's subject matter and the composition of Russell's *Indians Hunting Buffalo* (1894) is remarkably similar to Miller's *The Buffalo Hunt* (c1850).

In 1881, Russell finally embarked upon the career that would influence his art more than any other experience. After a short visit to his parents' home, he returned to the Judith Basin and joined the round-up as a horsewrangler, despite a slightly tarnished reputation as an employee. According to Russell, 'I was considered worthless an' was spoke of as "that 'onery Kid Russell".' Horsewrangling garnered little prestige but carried with it the great responsibility of

guarding the horses while the cowboys slept. In the fall of 1881, his outfit rehired him as a nightherder, a promotion of sorts; he now had to prevent the cattle from stampeding, a difficult job considering their unsettled nature. During the next 11 years, Russell lived the life of a cowboy: working grueling hours on dusty trails, sleeping on the open range and carousing and spending his wages in saloons. In these years, he would hone his knowledge of the Western landscape, cattle, horses and cowboys. By using the tin of watercolors he carried in his bedroll and any paper he could find, he translated his keen observations into increasingly beguiling sketches.

Russell began to work seriously with oils and larger canvases, the media for which he is best known, in 1885; for lack of a more appropriate setting, the artist used Jake Hoover's cabin or a saloon's backroom as a studio. His early attempts — *Breaking Camp* (1885) and *Cowboy Camp During Roundup* (c1887) — lack the tight composition, vivid detail and vibrant colors of paintings such as *The Herd Quitter* (1897) and *Utica* (1907), but they both contain the action and humor that would fill all his portrayals of cowboys.

TOP: Charles M. and Nancy C. Russell, wedding portrait, 1896.

ABOVE: Watercolor entitled *Waiting for a Chinook*.

FAR RIGHT: A postcard c.1890 showing American cowboys gambling – shooting craps (dice).

When the cattle drive was over in 1886, Russell settled at the O.H. Ranch where he helped to rescue the ranch's 5,000 cattle from 'the hardest winter the open range ever saw'. Russell dramatically depicted the tragedy of this winter in one of his most famous works, *Waiting for a Chinook* (1886). This watercolor is visually stark, but its emaciated steer and hungry, expectant wolves evoked the emotion and loss inflicted by the cruel blizzards of 1886 and 1887. Three hundred Westerners and over a million head of cattle died that winter, waiting for the warm wind called the Chinook. The survivors, touched by Russell's perceptive portrayal, circulated reproductions of the poignant watercolor throughout the United States; it was the first time his work was admired outside Montana, where newspapers already called him the 'Cowboy Artist'.

After the 1888 spring roundup, Russell accompanied two cowboy friends on a trip across the border to Canada where he accepted an offer to live with the Bloods, a Native American tribe belonging to the Blackfeet Nation. In the six months that Russell spent with the tribe, he gained a knowledge of their habits, traditions, myths and religion, all of which became subjects of his paintings and models. Russell's view of the Indians had changed dramatically, no longer were they the violent savages he and his friends had pretended to be in childhood games. Defending the Indians he once said: 'I've known some bad Injuns but for every bad one I kin

match 'im with ten worse white men . . . No Injun ever done me dirt. Many a one's done me favors. When he's a good friend, he's the best friend in the world.'

Although Russell painted the brutality of Native American life in paintings such as *Counting Coup* (1902) and *When Blackfeet and Sioux Meet* (1908), he also recorded the softer side of their existence in gentle scenes like *The Marriage Ceremony* (1894) and *Three Generations* (1897). Native American women are among Russell's few female characters, and they radiate strength and wisdom in his paintings and sculpture, such as the *Piegan Maiden* (c1910). Unlike the paintings of his contemporary Frederic Remington, which celebrated the American military's winning of the West from the Indian, Russell's paintings lamented the pain and tragedy suffered by his Indian friends. His depiction of historical events from the Native Americans' point of view was unique. In *Lewis and Clark Meeting the Indians at Ross' Hole* (1912), the white men are just visible in the background while the noble figures of the Native Americans fill the canvas, emphasizing the fact that they were the rightful inhabitants of the land.

Upon leaving the Bloods in the spring of 1889, Russell returned to Montana and his life as a cowboy. To supplement his meager wages, he sold his paintings in saloons to people he termed 'suckers'. Russell found it difficult to believe that his paintings and models, which gave him so much pleasure to

17

ABOVE: Cowboys eating at a chuckwagon.

LEFT: Colonel William Frederick Cody, aka "Buffalo Bill," from a picture post-card dated 27 April 1903.

BELOW: A poster for Buffalo Bill's Wild West show, 1898.

RIGHT: *Buffalo Dance of the Mandan*, a painting by Karl Bodmer during an expedition to the Far West in 1833-4.

COLONEL CODY "BUFFALO BILL"

COL. W. F. CODY "BUFFALO BILL"

create, were actually worth the five or ten dollars people were willing to pay for them. But he didn't complain when he and his many friends — all equally ignorant of money management — needed new boots, food or another round of whisky.

The year 1895 marked a dramatic change in the carefree existence of the artist; it was then that he met and married Nancy Cooper, a native of Kentucky who was visiting family friends in Montana. The 31-year old Russell charmed the teenaged Nancy with what she described as his 'square shoulders and straight back . . . expression of honesty and understanding . . . artistic, sensitive hands . . . [and] his stories of Western life.' Cupid had 'bushwhacked' Charlie, and when his friends heard that he had given Nancy one of his horses, they knew that there was no hope for their bachelor friend: 'A man don't give a gal his hoss 'less'n he's plumb locoed 'bout 'er. He'll have to marry the gal now to git his hoss back.'

Fortunately for the couple's well-being, Nancy had an innate skill in business matters and realized that her husband's work was worth far more than 10 dollars. In 1896, at Nancy's suggestion, the newlyweds moved from Cascade to Great Falls, a

larger city with more opportunities to sell her husband's art. Russell's father, now proud of his son's increasingly lucrative occupation, sponsored the building of a house for the young couple and a log cabin studio for his son. Russell transformed his studio into a shrine of the Old West, filling it with Native American and cowboy paraphernalia, bear skins and buffalo skulls. From the time the cabin was built, Russell never completed a painting elsewhere.

There can be little doubt that without Nancy, Russell would have continued to produce slapdash paintings for the price of a few drinks and groceries. Russell insisted:

'The lady I trotted in double harness with was the best booster an' pardner a man ever had. She could convince anybody that I was the greatest artist in the world, an' that makes a feller work harder . . . if she hadn't prodded me, I wouldn't have done the work I did.'

In 1903, Nancy decided a trip to New York City would boost her husband's career, so they left Great Falls for 'the big camp'. Although they weren't as

successful as they had hoped in selling Russell's paintings from a rented basement gallery, Nancy was able to place Russell's sketches in books and popular magazines such as *Harper's Weekly*, *Scribner's*, *Life* and *Punch*. Charlie despised New York, 'there are too many tall tepees. I'd rather live in a place where I know somebody and where everybody is somebody.' Nevertheless, he and Nancy traveled to the metropolis nearly every year searching for the recognition and success that finally came in 1911 with his one-man exhibit at the Folsom Galleries entitled 'The West That Has Past'. Although he continued to think of himself strictly as an illustrator, Russell was now a world-recognized painter who captured the Old West with incredible skill and attention to detail. His early, primitive paintings had evolved into spectacular, focused compositions with an increasingly bold use of color.

In the following years, Russell's work delighted art and Western enthusiasts in cities throughout the United States and Canada; he and Nancy even traveled to London at the request of the Doré Galleries in 1914. With his burgeoning popularity,

Two paintings by contemporaries of Russell, *Attack at Dawn*, (ABOVE) by Charles Schreyvogel, depicting the U.S. Cavalry making a surprise raid on an Indian village; and *The Bronco Buster*, (RIGHT) painted by Frederic Remington c.1895.

wealth and exposure to new places and cultures, Russell's personality changed very little. He desperately missed Montana on his brief sojourns and always longed to return. Wherever he went, he sent letters – filled with sketches and jokes about the oddities of people outside the West – to his Montana friends. Russell also continued to be surprised at the prices people were willing to pay for his work. When a potential customer balked at the idea of paying $10,000 for one of Russell's paintings, the artist agreed, 'Damned if I think it's worth ten thousand dollars either.' Nevertheless, Nancy Russell got her full asking price.

By the end of Russell's career, the subjects of his paintings were long dead, their way of life changed by the advent of trains and farmers in the case of cowboys, and by the brutality of whites in the case of Indians. Russell was not ignorant of this

Riding a Broncho.

transformation nor his role in recording the past. He proclaimed, 'The West is dead. You may lose a sweetheart, but you won't forget her.' When he died of heart failure in 1926, Russell left behind over 3,000 sketches, illustrations, paintings and models all of which shone with his love of the Old West. Their subjects may have little to do with modern life, but the humor, adventurous spirit and artistic skill they depict continue to inspire.

It is fitting that Charlie's last oil painting was entitled *Trail's End* (1926?). He had lived a full life and traveled over many trails as a cowboy, artist and husband. A few months before he died, he expressed his contentment: 'Any man that can make a living doing what he likes is lucky, and I'm that. Any time I cash in now, I win.' Today, it is the viewers of Russell's work who win. Russell, a self-educated artist, focused his immense talent on the dying Old West and left behind a valuable historical record and a superior collection of art.

**Cowpunching Sometimes Spells Trouble** 1889
Oil on canvas, 26 x 41 in.
Sid Richardson Collection of Western Art, Fort Worth, TX

**Western Scene (The Shelton Saloon Painting)** c. 1885
Oil on wood panel, 17½ x 69 in.
Sid Richardson Collection of Western Art, Fort Worth, TX

**Cowboy Sport – Roping a Wolf** 1890
Oil on canvas, 20 x 35¾ in.
Sid Richardson Collection of Western Art, Fort Worth, TX

**Grubpile (The Evening Pipe)** 1890
Oil on canvas, 9⅝ x 16⅜ in.
Sid Richardson Collection of Western Art, Fort Worth, TX

**Waiting for a Chinook**
Oil on canvas, 20½ x 29 in.
Buffalo Bill Historical Center, Cody, WY.
Gift of Charles Ulrick and Josephine Bay Foundation, Inc.

**Seeking New Hunting Grounds
(Breaking Camp; Indian Women and Children on the Trail)** c. 1891
Oil on canvas, 23¾ x 35⅞ in.
Sid Richardson Collection of Western Art, Fort Worth, TX

**The Buffalo Runners** c. 1892
Oil on canvas, 27⅝ x 39⅜ in.
Sid Richardson Collection of Western Art, Fort Worth, TX

**Plunder On the Horizon (Indians Discover Prospectors)** 1893
Oil on canvas, 24 x 36 in.
Sid Richardson Collection of Western Art, Fort Worth, TX

**There May Be Danger Ahead (Hunting Party on Mountain Trail)** 1893
Oil on canvas, 36¼ x 22 in.
Sid Richardson Collection of Western Art, Fort Worth, TX

**Trouble On The Horizon (Prospectors Discover an Indian Camp)** 1893
Oil on canvas, 26⅛ x 34 in.
Sid Richardson Collection of Western Art, Fort Worth, TX

**Attack On The Mule Train (Mule Pack Train)** 1894
Oil on canvas, 23⅛ x 35⅛ in.
Sid Richardson Collection of Western Art, Fort Worth, TX

**The Marriage Ceremony (Indian Love Call)** 1894
Oil on cardboard, 18½ x 24⅝ in.
Sid Richardson Collection of Western Art, Fort Worth, TX

**Indians Hunting Buffalo (Wild Men's Meat)** 1894
Oil on canvas, 24⅛ x 36⅛ in.
Sid Richardson Collection of Western Art, Fort Worth, TX

**Bringing Up the Trail** 1895
Oil on canvas, 22⅞ x 35 in.
Sid Richardson Collection of Western Art, Fort Worth, TX

**Three Generations** 1897
Oil on canvas, 17⅛ x 24¼ in.
Sid Richardson Collection of Western Art, Fort Worth, TX

**Captain William Clark of the Lewis and Clark Expedition
Meeting with the Indians of the Northwest** 1897
Oil on canvas, 29½ x 41½ in.
Sid Richardson Collection of Western Art, Fort Worth, TX

**The Ambush (The Road Agents)** 1896
Oil on canvas, 26⅛ x 35 in.
Sid Richardson Collection of Western Art, Fort Worth, TX

**The Buffalo Hunt (Wild Meat for Wild Men)** 1899
Oil on canvas, 24⅛ x 36⅛ in.
Sid Richardson Collection of Western Art, Fort Worth, TX

**When Cowboys Get In Trouble (The Mad Cow)** 1899
Oil on canvas, 24 x 36 in.
Sid Richardson Collection of Western Art, Fort Worth, TX

**Wild Man's Meat (Redman's Meat)** 1899
Pencil, watercolor and gouache on paper, 21 x 30 in.
Sid Richardson Collection of Western Art, Fort Worth, TX

**Breaking Up The Ring (Breaking Up The Circle)** 1900
Pencil, watercolor, and gouache on paper, 19½ x 29⅜ in.
Sid Richardson Collection of Western Art, Fort Worth, TX

**The Tenderfoot** 1900
Oil on canvas, 14⅛ x 20⅛ in.
Sid Richardson Collection of Western Art, Fort Worth, TX

**Returning To Camp** 1901
Oil on canvas, 24⅛ x 36 in.
Sid Richardson Collection of Western Art, Fort Worth, TX

**Buffalo Hunt** 1901
Oil on canvas, 24⅛ x 36⅛ in.
Sid Richardson Collection of Western Art, Fort Worth, TX

**Counting Coup (Medicine Whip)** 1902
Oil on canvas, 18⅛ x 30⅛ in.
Sid Richardson Collection of Western Art, Fort Worth, TX

**Trouble Hunters** 1902
Oil on canvas, 22 x 29⅛ in.
Sid Richardson Collection of Western Art, Fort Worth, TX

**The Bucker** 1904
Pencil, watercolor and gouache on paper, 16¼ x 12¼ in.
Sid Richardson Collection of Western Art, Fort Worth, TX

**He Snaked Old Texas Pete Right Out Of His Wicky-Up, Gun and All** 1905
Pencil, watercolor and gouache on paper, 12⅜ x 17⅛ in.
Sid Richardson Collection of Western Art, Fort Worth, TX

**The Scout** 1907
Pencil, watercolor and gouache on paper, 16¾ x 11⅝ in.
Sid Richardson Collection of Western Art, Fort Worth, TX

**Utica (A Quiet Day in Utica)**  1907
Oil on canvas, 24⅛ x 36⅛ in.
Sid Richardson Collection of Western Art, Fort Worth, TX

**When Blackfeet and Sioux Meet** 1908
Oil on canvas, 20½ x 29⅞ in.
Sid Richardson Collection of Western Art, Fort Worth, TX

**First Wagon Trail (First Wagon Tracks)** 1908
Pencil, watercolor and gouache on paper, 18¼ x 27 in.
Sid Richardson Collection of Western Art, Fort Worth, TX

**Wounded (The Wounded Buffalo)** 1909
Oil on canvas, 19⅞ x 30⅛ in.
Sid Richardson Collection of Western Art, Fort Worth, TX

**His Wealth (Braves On The March)** c. 1910
Pencil, watercolor and gouache on paper, 6¼ x 9¼ in.
Sid Richardson Collection of Western Art, Fort Worth, TX

**Portrait of an Indian** c. 1902
Oil on canvas, 10½ x 8 in.
Courtesy of the Montana Historical Society, Museum Purchase

**The Jerkline** 1912
Oil on canvas, 24 x 36 in.
C. M. Russell Museum, Great Falls, MT

**Paying The Fiddler** 1916
Oil on canvas, 24 x 36 in.
C. M. Russell Museum, Great Falls, MT

**A Bad One** 1912
Pencil, watercolor and gouache on paper, 19¾ x 28⅝ in.
Sid Richardson Collection of Western Art, Fort Worth, TX

**Toll Collectors** 1913
Oil on canvas, 24 x 36 in.
Courtesy of the Montana Historical Society, Mackay Collection

**The Roundup No 2** 1913
Oil on canvas, 25 x 49 in.
Courtesy of the Montana Historical Society, Mackay Collection

**When The Land Belonged To God** 1914
Oil on canvas, 42½ x 72 in.
Courtesy of the Montana Historical Society, Museum Purchase

**When Horses Talk War There's Small Chance for Peace** 1915
Oil on canvas, 24 x 36 in.
Courtesy of the Montana Historical Society, Mackay Collection

**Deer In Forest (White Tailed Deer)** 1917
Oil on canvasboard, 14 x 9⅞ in.
Sid Richardson Collection of Western Art, Fort Worth, TX

**Buffalo Bill's Duel With Yellowhand** 1917
Oil on canvas, 29⅞ x 47⅞ in.
Sid Richardson Collection of Western Art, Fort Worth, TX

**The Fireboat** 1918
Oil on board, 16 x 25 in.
C. M. Russell Museum, Great Falls, MT

**Signal Smoke** c. 1890
Oil on canvas, 24 x 36 in.
C. M. Russell Museum, Great Falls, MT

**Man's Weapons are Useless When Nature Goes Armed
(Weapons Of The Weak; Two Of A Kind Win)** 1916
Oil on canvas, 30 x 48⅛ in.
Sid Richardson Collection of Western Art, Fort Worth, TX

**When White Men Turn Red** 1922
Oil on canvas, 24 x 36¼ in.
Sid Richardson Collection of Western Art, Fort Worth, TX

**Men Of The Open Range** 1923
Oil on canvas, 24 x 36 in.
Courtesy of the Montana Historical Society, Mackay Collection

**Meat's Not Meat 'Till It's In The Pan**
Oil on canvas, 21½ x 16⅝ in.
The Thomas Gilcrease Institute of American History and Art
Tulsa, OK

**White Man's Buffalo** 1919
Oil on canvas, 14½ x 24 in.
The Thomas Gilcrease Institute of American History and Art
Tulsa, OK

**Bruin Not Bunny Turned the Leaders** 1924
Oil on canvas, 24⅜ x 36½ in.
The Thomas Gilcrease Institute of American History and Art
Tulsa, OK

**Jerked Down** 1907
Oil on canvas, 23 x 36¾ in.
The Thomas Gilcrease Institute of American History and Art
Tulsa, OK

**Lewis and Clark Meeting Indians at Ross' Hole** 1912
Oil on canvas, 25 x 12ft.
Courtesy of the Montana Historical Society

**Keeoma No 3** 1898
Oil on canvas, 17½ x 23½in.
Courtesy of the Montana Historical Society, Museum Purchase

**Joe Kipp's Trading Post** 1898
Watercolour and gouache over pencil, 11¹³⁄₁₆ x 18 in.
Buffalo Bill Historical Center, Cody, WY
Gift by exchange from Charles Ulrick and Josephine Bay Foundation, Inc.

**Indians on a Bluff Surveying General Miles' Troops**
Oil on canvas, 23 x 35½ in.
Buffalo Bill Historical Center, Cody, WY
Gift of William E. Weiss

**Roping a Grizzly** 1903
Watercolour on paper, 19½ x 28½ in.
Buffalo Bill Historical Center, Cody, WY
Gift of William E. Weiss

**Where Great Herds Come To Drink** 1901
Oil on canvas, 30 x 36 in.
Buffalo Bill Historical Center, Cody, WY

**His Heart Sleeps** 1911
Oil on canvas, 6⅞ x 11⅞ in.
Buffalo Bill Historical Center, Cody, WY
Gift of the Charles Ulrick and Josephine Bay Foundation, Inc.

**Trail's End**
Oil on canvas, 15¼ x 21⅛ in.
Buffalo Bill Historical Center, Cody, WY
Charles Ulrick and Josephine Bay
Foundation, Inc.

**The Buffalo Herd**
Oil on board, 17¾ x 23¾ in.
Buffalo Bill Historical Center, Cody, WY
Gift of William E. Weiss

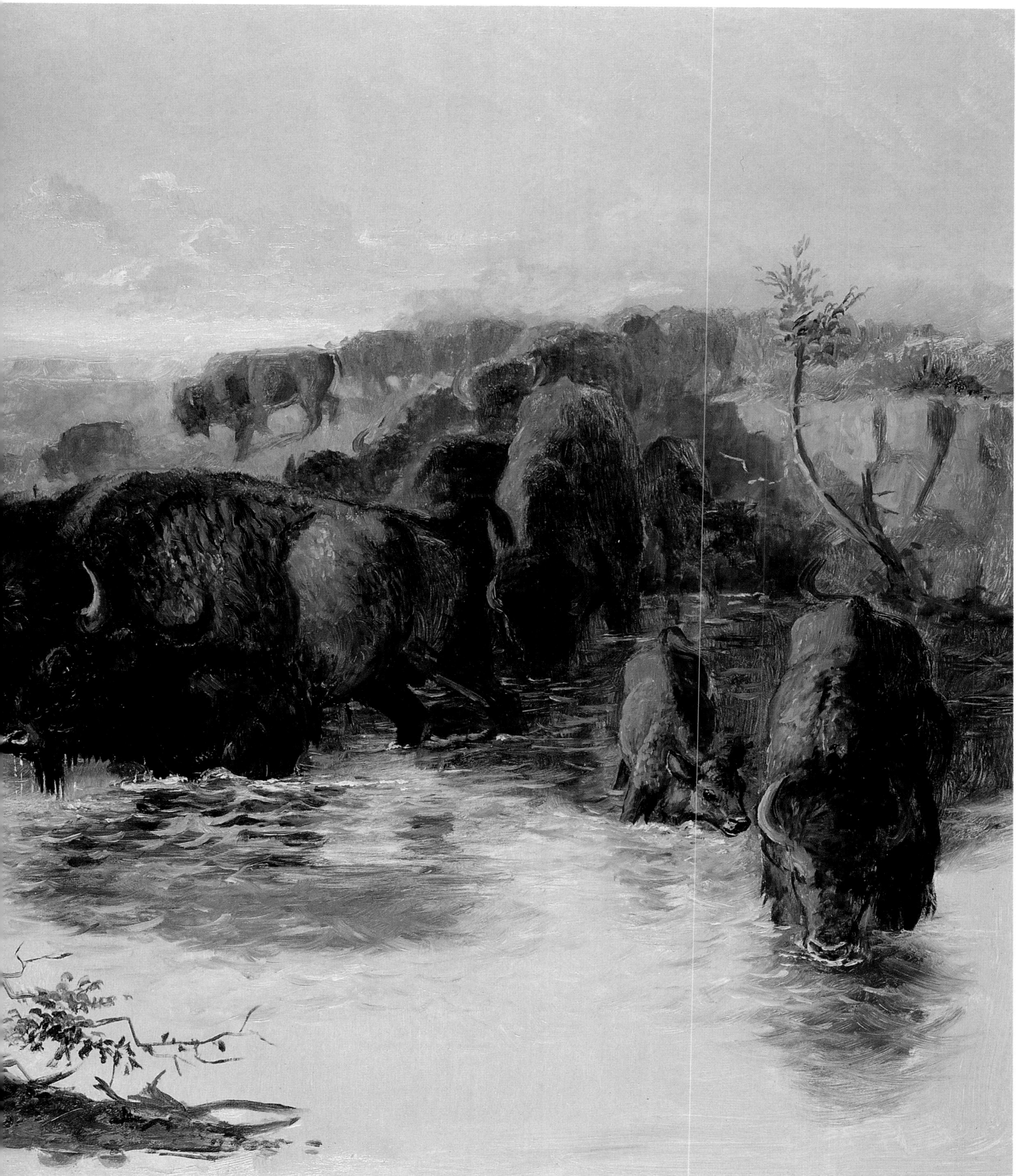

**The Battle** 1905
Watercolour on paper, 13½ x 19⅜ in.
Buffalo Bill Historical Center, Cody, WY
Gift of William E. Weiss

# SCULPTURES

**Piegan Maiden**
Bronze
C. M. Russell Museum, Great Falls, MT

**The Scalp Dancer**
Bronze
The Thomas Gilcrease Institute of American History and Art
Tulsa, OK

**The Secrets of the Night**
Bronze
The Thomas Gilcrease Institute of American History and Art
Tulsa, OK

**The Mountain Mother**
Bronze
The Thomas Gilcrease Institute of American History and Art
Tulsa, OK

**The Indian Family**
Bronze
The Thomas Gilcrease Institute of American History and Art
Tulsa, OK

**The Bronc Twister** 1963 cast
Bronze
C. M. Russell Museum, Great Falls, MT

**The Medicine Whip**
Bronze
The Thomas Gilcrease Institute of American History and Art
Tulsa, OK

# ACKNOWLEDGEMENTS

**The Author and Publisher gratefully acknowledge the permission granted by the following organisations to publish the illustrations on the following pages:**

Peter Newark's Western Americana, Bath
17, 18 (All), 19, 20, 21, 22 (both), 23

Buffalo Bill Historical Center, Cody, WY
13, 14 (Both), 16 (Below), 32/3, 110/1, 112/3,
114, 115, 116, 117, 118/9, 120

Sid Richardson Collection of Western Art, Fort
Worth, TX
1, 2, 4, 7, 9, 15, 24/5, 26/7, 28/9, 30/1, 34/5,
36/7, 38/9, 40, 41, 42/3, 44/5, 46/7, 48/9, 50/1,
52/3, 54/5, 56/7, 58/9, 60, 61, 62/3, 64/5, 66/7,
68/9, 70, 71, 72, 73, 74/5, 76/7, 78/9, 80/1, 82,
87, 94, 95, 99, 100/1

C. M. Russell Museum, Great Falls, MT
11, 12, 16 (Top), 84/5, 86, 96/7, 98, 121, 126

The Thomas Gilcrease Institute of American
History and Art Tulsa, OK
104, 105, 106, 107, 122, 123, 124, 125, 127

The Montana Historical Society, Helena, MT
8, 83, 88, 89, 90/1, 92/3, 102/3, 108, 109